Celebrate Thanksgiving

Charlene Notgrass

Celebrate Thanksgiving

Design and Content by Charlene Notgrass

ISBN 978-1-933410-18-0

Notgrass company

Curriculum That Teaches the Heart, Soul, and Mind

975 Roaring River Road
Gainesboro, TN 38562
1-800-211-8793
www.notgrass.com
books@notgrass.com

Contents

How to Use *Celebrate Thanksgiving*

Thanksgiving brings to mind Pilgrims and Native Americans, turkey and pumpkin pie, football games and going to Grandma's house — and most importantly, giving thanks to God for His blessings. Why do we celebrate this annual holiday in America? This study explores answers to this question.

What's included in *Celebrate Thanksgiving*?

- Fifteen lessons of four pages each in which students discover information about Thanksgiving. The lessons explore history, geography, Bible study, art, poetry, grammar, creative writing, character, science, traditions, and thinking skills.
- Craft instructions for seven projects.
- A Thanksgiving scrapbook (the paper in *Celebrate Thanksgiving* is acid-free).

How many copies of *Celebrate Thanksgiving* do I need for my family?

One per child. Students learn about Thanksgiving as they read and complete activities in the curriculum. They also complete a Thanksgiving scrapbook, which is included at the back of the curriculum.

How long does it take to complete this curriculum?

Each lesson takes about 30 minutes to an hour. Here are three possible schedules:

Complete one lesson per day (Monday through Friday) beginning three full weeks before the week of Thanksgiving. During the week of Thanksgiving, complete craft projects and the scrapbook.

Complete one lesson per day (Monday through Friday) beginning three full weeks before the week of Thanksgiving and do one or two craft projects each week. During the week of Thanksgiving, complete more craft projects and the scrapbook.

Complete one lesson every other day (Monday through Friday) beginning six full weeks before the week of Thanksgiving and do one craft project each week, including the week of Thanksgiving. Complete scrapbook during Thanksgiving weekend.

A Note About the Creative Writing

Children should follow these steps in their creative writing:

1. Write the assignment on regular paper first.
2. Proofread their writing.
3. Ask parents to check their writing.
4. Make corrects or rewrite the assignment, if needed (also followed by proofreading, a parent check, and corrections).
5. Copy their writing into the *Celebrate Thanksgiving* workbook.

Note: The heirloom table cloth must be completed during your Thanksgiving celebration. See page 71 for details. Ours is pictured on the back cover.

How can I make the study even more memorable?

Costumes. Use your imagination to come up with some Pilgrim costumes. You don't have to make anything elaborate. We have found really great costume components at thrift stores. Sew some white ribbon on a white handkerchief and you have an instant bonnet. On the other hand, older children might really enjoy sewing costumes for themselves and their younger siblings. Your children could wear the

costumes on Thanksgiving Day, on some special occasion, or, if it is not too distracting, wear them every day while they study *Celebrate Thanksgiving*.

Make-believe. You can pretend to sail on the *Mayflower*. Write *Mayflower* on a piece of paper and tape it to the headboard of a big bed (or have one of

One year our family had fun making costumes. John, Mary Evelyn, and Bethany wore their costumes to a homeschool Thanksgiving program.

your children draw the *Mayflower* and make a nice poster). Find some good library books about Pilgrims. While you are studying *Celebrate Thanksgiving*, spend some time each day reading on the bed. Explain to your children that the bed is the *Mayflower* and that you are going to experience living in really tight quarters, like the Pilgrims did while on their "ship." Have your children think about how long the Pilgrims had to travel to get to their new home in America.

More make-believe. Get a blue sheet and a toy plastic boat. Pretend that the boat is the Mayflower and it is being tossed by the waves of the Atlantic Ocean. Simply have your family gather around and hold the sheet by the corners and sides. Put the boat in the middle and gently toss it up and down.

Liz and Hannah enjoy their candy and cookie turkeys. See page 68 for directions.

I really love Thanksgiving. It has long been a favorite holiday for me. Perhaps one reason is that in 1975 when my husband Ray and I had been married not quite a year, I had to work on the Friday after Thanksgiving. We decided it was too hard to make the drive back home to Tennessee. I called my Mama Sue (my Daddy's mother) and asked her how to make turkey and dressing. At the ripe old age of 21, I cooked my first turkey. I was hooked! We had a great Thanksgiving with other friends who were away from home and began making our own Thanksgiving traditions. These days we are back in Tennessee and able to have our own traditions and invite our extended family to our house. That's really special. I love to *Celebrate Thanksgiving*! I hope you enjoy it, too.

Charlene Notgrass

Thanksgiving Lessons

Lesson 1 — History, Spelling, Art, Bible Study, Grammar

Who Were the Pilgrims?

Some of the words in the paragraphs below are written backwards. Write them correctly. When you have finished filling in the blanks, read the lesson again.

After studying briefly at Cambridge University, William **RETSWERB** ________________ worked for an English ambassador and later as a baliff and a postmaster. In 1606, he and other Christians who believed differently from the Church of **DNALGNE** ______________ broke away from that church and became known as **STSITARAPES** ____________. King James I and his government **DETUCESREP** _____________ the Separatists. In 1608, Brewster led a group of them to The **SDNALREHTEN** _________________, so they could escape the persecution. In 1609, they settled in **NEDIEL** ________________ (pronounced lie-den and sometimes spelled Leyden).

While in The Netherlands, Brewster earned money by teaching and by publishing books. His books were **DENNAB** ____________ in England. The Separatists became discouraged when their **NERDLIHC** _______________ began to be influenced by people who lived around them. After the group had been in Leiden for several years, some of them **DETOV** ________________ to establish a colony in North America. William Brewster was among those who decided to

William Brewster lived in Scrooby, England. Scrooby is in Nottinghamshire, setting of the Robin Hood legends.

move to North America. Another Separatist who chose to **ETARGIME** ________________ was William **DROFDARB** __________________. Bradford was the first person to use the term **MIRGLIP** _____________ to describe these early religious **SRELTTES** ________________. He wrote a **YROTSIH** _____________ of their colony in America. His *History of Plimouth Plantation 1620-1647* helps historians know about the early years of the Pilgrims in the Plymouth Colony. Bradford was elected **RONREVOG** ______________ of their settlement thirty times and served as governor almost continuously from 1621 through 1656. William Brewster also served in a **PIHSREDAEL** _______________________ role when the Separatists moved to America.

Thinking about the Lesson

Notice the painting of William Brewster at left. From where is the light shining?

____

Why did the artist paint the light that way? __________

____

____

____

____

Why did the artist turn Brewster's right hand upward?

____

____

____

This painting, "Landing of the Pilgrims," was created by Italian artist Constantino Brumidi. This and eighteen other scenes from American history decorate the Rotunda of the United States Capitol. The painting depicts William Brewster thanking God for the safe landing of the Pilgrims.

Psalm 100

Psalm 100 is often associated with Thanksgiving Day. The following translation of Psalm 100 is from the King James Bible, which was published in 1611, just three years after the Separatists moved to the Netherlands. Read the Psalm and color the illustration.

Make a joyful noise unto the Lord, all ye lands.
Serve the Lord with gladness:
come before his presence with singing.
Know ye that the Lord he is God:
it is he that hath made us, and not we ourselves;
we are his people, and the sheep of his pasture.
Enter into his gates with thanksgiving,
and into his courts with praise:
be thankful unto him,
and bless his name.
For the Lord is good;
his mercy is everlasting;
And his truth endureth
to all generations.

Prepositional Phrases in Psalm 100

A prepositional phrase begins with a preposition (such as to, with, of, or unto).
A prepositional phrase ends with a noun (a person, place, or thing).
It may also include other words that describe or identify the noun (like his, the, or all).
Finish these statements using a prepositional phrase from Psalm 100. Write one word in each blank.

1. We should make a joyful noise __________ __________ __________.
2. We should serve the Lord __________ ____________________.
3. We should come before his presence __________ ____________________.
4. We are the sheep __________ __________ ____________________.
5. We should enter into his gates __________ ____________________.
6. We should enter into his courts __________ ____________________.
7. The Lord's truth endures __________ __________ ____________________.

The printed statements above include three more prepositional phrases, in addition to the ones that you have copied from Psalm 100. Finish them below.

__________ _____ presence

__________ _____ gates

__________ _____ courts

Lesson 2 — History, Puzzle, Rhyming, Science, Creative Writing

The Pilgrims of the Plymouth Colony and Their Native American Neighbors

In September of 1620, William Brewster, William Bradford, and other Separatists (later known as **PILGRIMS**), plus other people whom they considered "strangers," gathered in Plymouth, **ENGLAND**. They stepped aboard the ***MAYFLOWER*** and traveled across the **ATLANTIC** Ocean to settle in **AMERICA**. While they were sailing to America, a baby boy was born — Oceanus Hopkins. While still on the ship, they wrote rules by which to live in their new home. This document was called the Mayflower **COMPACT**.

When the Pilgrims arrived in America to build their **COLONY** and serve God in freedom, they explored part of the coast of what is now **MASSACHUSETTS**. They chose land along **PLYMOUTH** Bay. The land had once belonged to the **PATUXET** Indians. The Pilgrims landed at the site of present-day Plymouth on December 21, 1620.

The settlers began to build Plymouth Colony. Over half of them died during their difficult first winter. **SQUANTO** of the Patuxet tribe helped the colonists survive. He had been to England and spoke **ENGLISH** well. Squanto taught the settlers how to plant corn, where to find fish and other food, served as a guide, and helped work out a peace **TREATY** between the Plymouth colonists and the **WAMPANOAG**

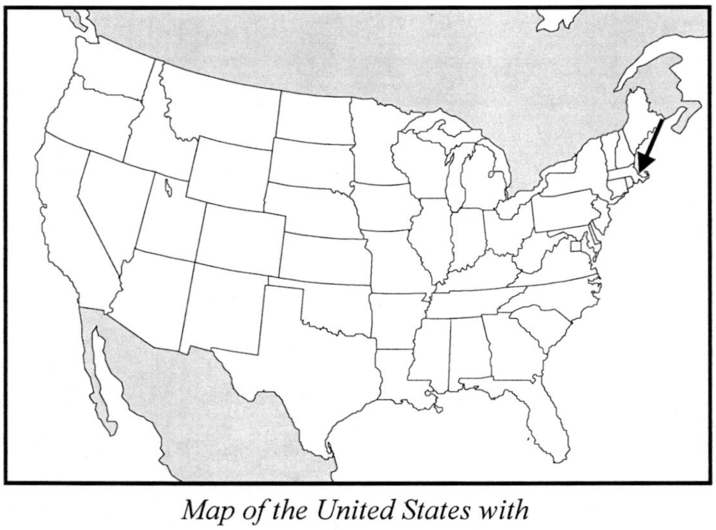

Map of the United States with arrow pointing toward Plymouth

tribe living nearby. Squanto lived with the Plymouth settlers until his death. Before he died, he asked Governor William **BRADFORD** to pray for him "that he might go to the Englishmen's God in heaven." The Pilgrims and the Wampanoag lived together as peaceful neighbors for 50 years.

*In the puzzle below, circle the capitalized **WORDS** from pages 6 and 7.*

P	A	M	A	S	S	A	C	H	U	S	E	T	T	S	P
Q	I	T	A	M	E	L	R	X	D	C	K	B	T	B	Q
E	P	L	L	Y	E	F	M	S	Y	E	O	L	R	E	C
U	N	L	G	A	F	R	G	N	T	W	A	M	P	A	N
O	A	G	Y	R	N	L	I	H	O	U	Z	F	P	M	D
G	D	N	L	M	I	T	O	C	O	L	O	N	Y	A	N
F	L	E	T	A	O	M	I	W	A	I	P	V	A	G	C
O	O	I	F	O	N	U	S	C	E	K	J	Q	W	B	H
T	P	R	S	G	J	D	T	A	T	R	E	A	T	Y	C
I	J	Q	D	H	H	K	M	H	B	C	D	P	A	T	U
X	E	T	R	S	A	I	L	N	O						

This painting by an unknown artist has this caption:

After gathering in a plentiful harvest to tide them over the next long winter, the Pilgrims dedicated to Providence a day of public Thanksgiving.

Learning About Corn

The Pilgrims learned about corn from Native Americans. You can learn about corn in these paragraphs, but you will have to do some work first. The words in all capital letters are incorrect. When you come to an incorrect word, cross it out and write the correct word in the blank beside it. The correct words are listed in bold type below. When you have finished filling in the blanks correctly, read the lesson again. Pictured at the bottom right are two ears of Indian corn. The shucks have been pulled back to reveal the corn kernels. Color the dried shucks beige and the kernels shades of gold and yellow.

STALK GRAIN EAR FOOD MEAL COB RICE CHIPS
SHELLS WHEAT FLAKES KERNELS STEM

A crop of corn. Notice the stalks and leaves.

Today corn, **MICE** _________, and **SHEET** ____________ are the three main grains grown in the world. Corn is native to North and South America and is the largest **MANE** _________ crop grown in the United States. The corn plant has a straight, solid **GEM** __________ (called a **WALK** _______) and long thin leaves. Ears of corn grow on these stalks. Each **DEER** _______ of corn has about one thousand **COLONELS** ___________ on a long thin **KNOB** ______ . Green husks completely cover the kernels.

Corn is used as **DUDE** _______ for people and for animals. Factories make corn into many products, like corn **SHIPS** ___________ , taco **BELLS** _________ , corn **STEAKS** _________, corn **WHEEL** _______ , and corn syrup. Families use meal to make corn bread and spoon bread and factories use corn syrup in many processed foods.

A Prayer of Thanksgiving

Pretend you are a Pilgrim in the Plymouth Colony. On a separate piece of paper, write a prayer of Thanksgiving for the blessings of your life in the Plymouth Colony. After you and your parent make corrections, copy it onto this page.

Lesson 3 – History, Geography, Puzzle

Two Plymouths: One in England...

Today's lesson tells about the Plymouth from which the Pilgrims sailed and the new Plymouth they began in America. Ships are of central importance in the history of Plymouth, England. One or more letters of the word **S H I P** *are missing from some of the words in these paragraphs. As you read through the paragraphs, fill in the missing letters. When you have finished filling in the blanks, read the lesson again.*

__lymouth, England is located on the __outhern coast in the county of Devon. The geographic region is also called Devonshire. Before Plymouth received its town charter in 1439, it was named Sutton. The town lies along the waterways of the River Plym, the River Tamar, and the Engl__ __h Channel. It has a fine natural __arbor.

Statue of Sir Francis Drake in Plymouth, England

Before the __ilgrims __ailed from __lymouth in 1620, the town had been the departure point for other __istoric __ailing ventures. Frances Drake __ailed from __lymouth in 1577. He traveled from there to __outh America, where he fought against __pain. In 1581, he became the mayor of __lymouth. He was knighted by Queen Elizabeth I that same year, becoming __ir Frances Drake. Conflict with __pain continued and in 1588 a fleet of 130 __panish __ __ __ __s, called the __panish Armada, tried to invade England. The English fleet __et __ail from __lymouth to meet them. The English fleet defeated the __panish Armada.

Map of the island of Great Britain with arrow pointing toward Plymouth

During World War II, German __lanes bombed __lymouth heavily. On June 6, 1944 Allied forces left England to begin the Normandy __nvasion, which eventually led to the defeat of Germany. More Allied troops followed after the first soldiers left on June 6. My father-in-law, Wesley Notgrass, __ailed from England to Normandy on June 7, the day after D-day. His group __ailed from Plymouth.

Water transportation continues to play an __mportant role in the commerce of __lymouth. __assenger vessels leave from __lymouth to take travelers to the European continent and it is a major f__ __hing __ort. __lymouth is the home of the United Kingdom's Royal Naval Dockyard.

Today the town has museums, an aquarium, a zoo, and the University of __lymouth. It's __opulation is about 250,000.

The Eddystone Lighthouse stands 13 miles southwest of Plymouth, England. This print from the Library of Congress was produced a few years after its construction in 1882. The small stump to the left is all that remains of the former Eddystone Lighthouse that stood from 1759 to 1882.

Fishing boats in Plymouth, England harbor, date unknown.

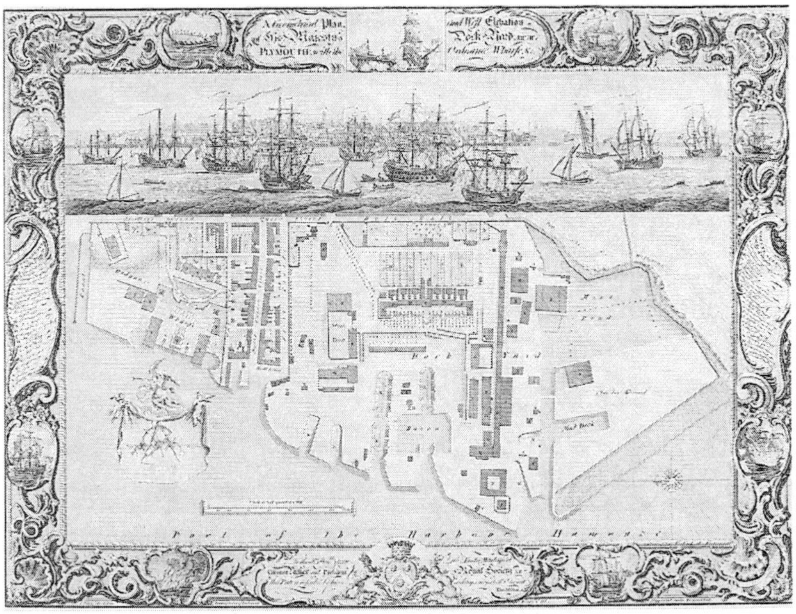

Map of Plymouth, England, in 1756

... And One in Massachusetts

A drawing of Plymouth and Plymouth Bay, dating from the early 1800s.

Captain John Smith is often remembered because of his work to establish the Jamestown colony in 1607 and because of his association with Pocahontas. In addition to the Jamestown colony, Smith helped encourage other English colonization in America. In 1614, he and his crew explored and mapped the northeastern coast of what is now the United States. He was the first to the call the area New England. In 1616, he published *A Description of New England*. A map in the book labels Plymouth Bay. The **Pilgrims**, who landed there in 1620, named their settlement Plymouth.

Leyden Street, Plymouth.

The first families in Plymouth built houses along one street that went from Fort Hill down to the sea. By the time this drawing was created, the street was known as Leyden Street. It is still Leyden Street today.

Plymouth, **Massachusetts**, like Plymouth, England, is a **fishing** center, but its main business is **tourism**. It is home to the *Mayflower II*, a full-size **replica** of the original ***Mayflower***, and to Plimoth Plantation, a living history village. Plimoth Plantation was recreated to depict Plymouth in 1627. The village has actors who portray particular individuals who lived there at that time; rare animal breeds, including ones living in New England in the 1600s; and crops like those grown by the Pilgrims. The tourist attraction also has a **Wampanoag** village, which depicts lives of Native Americans living nearby.

While in Plymouth, visitors can also see Burial Hill Cemetery, with its graves of original Pilgrims; homes dating to the 1600s; and Plymouth **Rock**. Plymouth Rock is probably not what the original settlers saw, but for many years it has been a symbol of the Pilgrims' landing.

In the paragraphs above, some words are underlined. Fit them into the puzzle below.

Daniel Webster (1782-1852) served in the U.S. House of Representatives, in the U.S. Senate, and as Secretary of State, but he is most famous for his speeches, especially the one he gave in Plymouth on December 22, 1820, in commemoration of the Bicentennial of the founding of Plymouth.

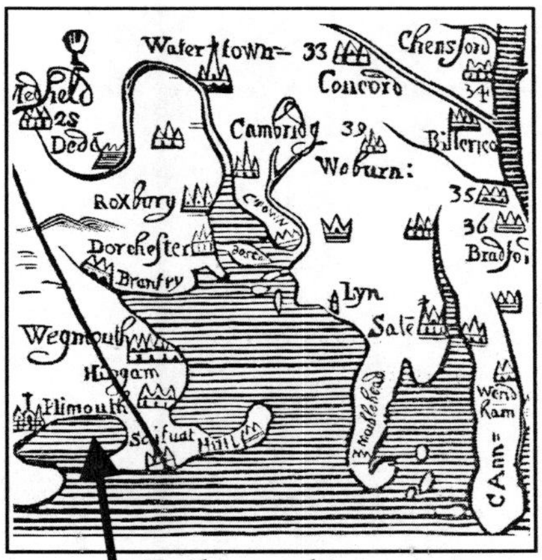

Early woodcut map showing Plimouth.

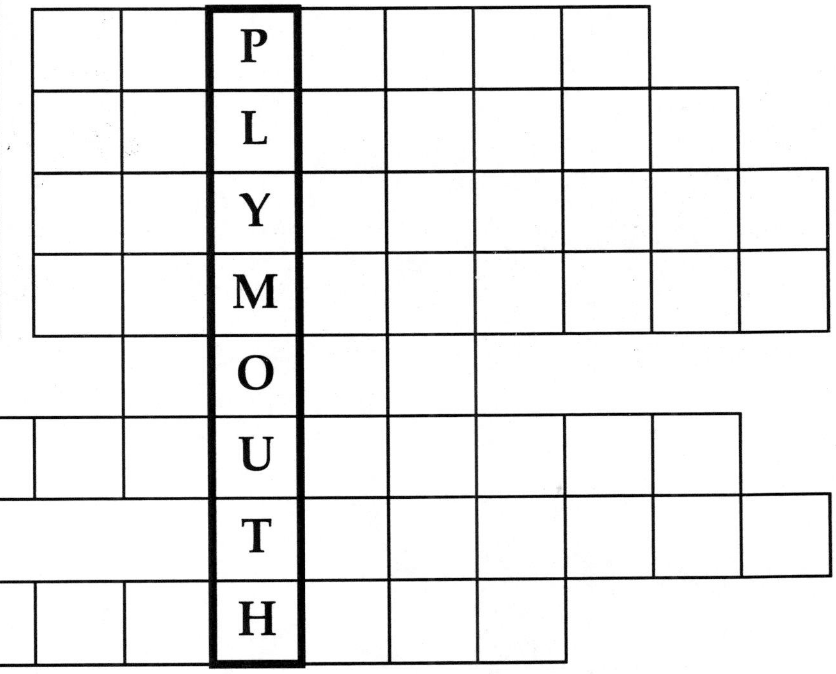

This monument houses Plymouth Rock.

Plymouth Rock

Lesson 4 - History, Art, Creative Writing, Bible Study, Puzzle, Science

A Gathering of Pilgrims and Native Americans in 1621

In the paragraph below, some words are scrambled. Here is an unscrambled list of those words. Fill in each blank with the correct unscrambled word. When you have finished filling in the blanks, read the lesson again.

RECREATION TRIBE PLYMOUTH GIFTS HARVEST HUNTING AUTUMN FEASTING CELEBRATION GOVERNOR FOWL CHIEF DEER PILGRIMS

In the **UNUMAT** __________ of 1621 the **MIRSGIPL** ___________ of **OLPTMYHU** ___________ gathered in their **VRHATES** _____________. According to a letter written by Edward Winslow in 1621, **EVOGRRON** _____________ William Bradford sent four men **TNUHGNI** __________________ for **WLFO** _________ so that they could have a special time of rejoicing. During the celebration, the Pilgrims enjoyed **SAEFGNIT** __________________ and **TAERNOIRCE** __________________, including "exercising their arms." They hosted about 90 men of the Wampanoag **BERTI** ________________, including their **EHCFI** ________________ Massasoit, for three days of **OTREENCIABL** _________________. During the feasting, the Wampanoags went hunting and brought back five **ERDE** _____________ as **FGSTI** _____________ for Pilgrim leaders.

An Artist's View of the Feast

In the early 1900s, Jean Leon Gerome Ferris (1863-1930) created a series of historical paintings called the Pageant of a Nation. His depiction of the gathering of the Pilgrims and Indians in 1621 is shown below. On a separate piece of paper, write a detailed description of his painting. Describe the setting, the people, and their activities. After you and your parent make corrections, copy it onto this page.

God Gives the Harvest

The Pilgrims and Native Americans celebrated the autumn harvest. God has promised that there will always be a harvest time. He made this promise after Noah and his family left the ark.

Scarecrows have become symbols of autumn and harvest time in America.

Read God's promise and color the scarecrow.

While the earth remains,
Seedtime and harvest,
And cold and heat,
And summer and winter,
And day and night
Shall not cease.

Genesis 8:22

Learning about Cranberries

Many Americans and Canadians include cranberries in their Thanksgiving celebrations (Canadians celebrate Thanksgiving on the second Monday in October). God has created several **types** of cranberries. The deep **red** cranberry usually associated with Thanksgiving is the **American** cranberry, which is native to eastern North America from the mountains of North Carolina northward into Canada.

Cranberry harvest of an earlier time. Today cranberries are harvested by machines.

Cranberries grow on a perennial evergreen **vine** which first produces pink flowers and then a white **fruit**, which later becomes deep red. White cranberry **juice** is made from cranberries that are **ripe** but have not yet turned red. God has made cranberries highly nutritious. The **berry** contains antioxidants which help our bodies heal and stay healthy.

Most of the cranberries grown in the U.S. are grown in Wisconsin and Massachusetts. They are also grown commercially in Michigan, Minnesota, New Jersey, Oregon, Maine, and Washington. When it is time to harvest the berries, farmers flood the fields. This makes the fruit float to the top of the water where they can easily be harvested. Where temperatures are very cold, farmers flood the fields again in the winter to keep the plants from freezing. Only about 5% of cranberries are sold as fresh fruit. The rest are made into cranberry juice and juice drinks, cranberry **sauce**, and sweetened dried cranberries.

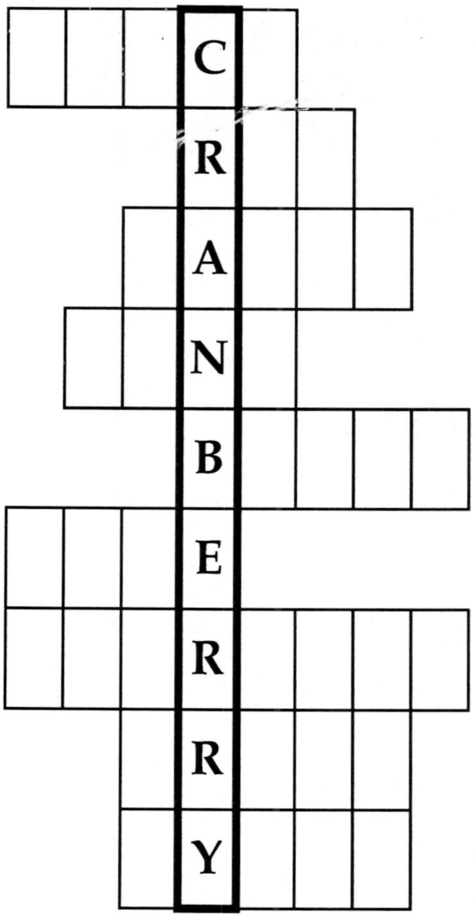

In the paragraphs above, some words are underlined. Fit them into the puzzle at left.

Cranberries in a field flooded and ready for the harvest.

The Thanksgiving Holiday Began in New England

The Pilgrims of Plymouth observed only three kinds of holidays. Each Sunday they observed the "Sabbath" by worshipping God and hearing sermons. They also held days of Fasting and Humiliation and days of Thanksgiving. The Pilgrims called for a day of Fasting and Humiliation when they felt God's hand of judgment and for a day of Thanksgiving when they saw special blessings. Days of Fasting or Thanksgiving were usually held on Thursday, the regular day for their mid-week church meeting. While the Pilgrims surely thanked God for their food in 1621, there is no record that the harvest celebration of that year was an official Thanksgiving for them.

The Pilgrims actually held their first official day of Thanksgiving during the summer of 1623 after God sent a rain that saved their crops. Governor Bradford wrote about the Indians' astonishment over this blessing from God. It was not until the 1800s that Americans began to refer to the Pilgrims' 1621 harvest celebration as the "first Thanksgiving."

Over the years settlements throughout New England began having annual Thanksgiving holidays during the autumn. Authorities in a community would simply announce a date and residents would start preparing for the celebration. By the middle of the 1600s, the custom of having an annual Thanksgiving was firmly established.

A Thanksgiving Hymn

"We Gather Together" is the traditional hymn of Thanksgiving. This hymn was written in Dutch by Adrianus Valerius in 1597 and was called "Wilt Heden Nu Treden." It was published in a Dutch hymnal in either 1621 or 1626, about the time that the first Dutch settlers arrived in America and founded New Amsterdam (later New York). The song was later translated into German. Theodore Baker translated the following version from German to English in 1894. Some of the verbs in this poem are written backwards. Write them correctly. When you have finished filling in the blanks, read the hymn. Write two definitions at the bottom of the page.

We Gather Together

We **REHTAG** ______________ together to ask the Lord's blessing.
He **SNETSAHC** ______________ and **SNETSAH** ______________ His will to make known.
The wicked oppressing now **ESAEC** ______________ from distressing.
GNIS ______________ praises to His name; He forgets not His own.

Beside us to guide us our God with us joining,
Ordaining, maintaining His kingdom divine.
So from the beginning the fight we were **GNINNIW** ______________.
Thou, Lord, **TSAW** ______________ at our side; all glory be Thine!

We all do **LOTXE** ______________ thee, Thou leader triumphant,
And **YARP** ______________ that Thou still our Defender wilt be.
Let thy congregation escape tribulation.
Thy name be ever **DESIARP** ______________! Oh, Lord, make us free.

Write the definition of these verbs:

Chasten - ____

____

Extol - ____

____

God's Word Teaches About Being Thankful

The Bible teaches us that all our blessings come from God. It teaches us about thankfulness and also gives us examples of people who gave thanks.

Write the letter of each question in the left column by its correct answer in the right column. Look up the Bible passages so you can answer the questions.

A. How long will the Psalmist give thanks to God? Psalm 30:12	☐	**Thanksgiving**
B. Where was Jonah when he promised to sacrifice with a song of thanksgiving? Jonah 2:9-10	☐	**Toward heaven**
C. Who gave thanks to God when she saw the infant Jesus? Luke 2:36-38	☐	**A Samaritan**
D. When Jesus fed the 5000 people, where did He look when He blessed the food? Mark 6:41	☐	**Cup**
E. Who thanked Jesus for healing him? Luke 17:11-19	☐	**In a fish**
F. When Jesus ate the Last Supper, He gave thanks when He took the what? Matthew 26:27	☐	**They recognized Jesus**
G. When we make requests of God, what else should we include in our prayers? Philippians 4:6	☐	**Anna**
H. After the resurrection, Jesus talked with two men walking to Emmaus. What happened when He took the bread, blessed it, broke it, and gave it to them? Luke 24:28-31	☐	**Forever**

Artists sometimes illustrate passages from the Bible. The pictures below illustrate five of the passages from lesson 5. The picture at the bottom left is quite different from the others, but it is still an effective illustration. The one in the middle is by the famous artist and scientist, Leonardo da Vinci. Write the correct Bible reference below each picture.

____

____

____

____

____

Thanksgiving During the American Revolution

In 1777, during the American Revolutionary War, the Continental Congress declared a day of Thanksgiving after the American victory over the British at the Battle of Saratoga. The Continental Congress declared a day of Thanksgiving every year through the end of the war in 1783.

In 1779, a young woman, Juliana Smith, wrote a letter to a friend telling about her family's Thanksgiving celebration. From this letter we learn how they celebrated and what foods they enjoyed at their feast.

Use this secret code to discover details about the Smith family's Thanksgiving celebration during the Revolutionary War. Think about how things have changed and how they have stayed the same. When you have finished filling in the blanks, read the statements again.

A = ▲ B = ▼ C = △ D = ▽ E = ⇨ F = ⇦ G = ♦ H = ❖
I = ↑ J = ↓ K = ✋ L = ✓ M = ☺ N = ⚐ O = ☼ P = ☜
Q = ☹ R = ☞ S = 🔔 T = < U = > V = ✂
W = ✎ X = # Y = * Z = ?

1. Before the meal, they went to ☺ ⇨ ⇨ < ↑ ⚐ ♦ ________________ to give thanks to God.
2. Family members took < > ☞ ⚐ 🔔 ________________ hosting the dinner each year.

3. Guests helped the host family by bringing
⇦ ☼ ☼ ▽ __________ .

4. 🔔 ⇨ ☞ ✂ ▲ ⚐ < 🔔 __________
served the host family and the guests who sat around tables in the dining room.

5. They celebrated with their ⇦ ▲ ☺ ↑ ✓ *
__________ .

6. They had no ▼ ⇨ ⇨ ⇦ __________ because all of it had to go to the ▲ ☞ ☺ * __________ .

7. Instead, they had ✂ ⇨ ⚐ ↑ 🔔 ☼ ⚐ __________ ,
☜ ↑ ♦ ⇨ ☼ ⚐ __________ ☜ ▲ 🔔 < ↑ ⇨ 🔔
__________ , ☜ ☼ ☞ ✋ __________ , < > ☞ ✋ ⇨ *
__________ , and ♦ ☼ ☼ 🔔 ⇨ __________ .

8. For dessert they had ☜ > ☺ ☜ ✋ ↑ ⚐ __________ pie, apple
< ▲ ☞ < 🔔 __________ , and ↑ ⚐ ▽ ↑ ▲ ⚐
__________ ☜ > ▽ ▽ ↑ ⚐ ♦ __________ .

9. While still at the table some of the men sang hymns and ▼ ▲ ✓ ✓ ▲ ▽ 🔔
__________ .

10. Then the group sang a ❖ * ☺ ⚐ __________ and were led in a
☜ ☞ ▲ * ⇨ ☞
__________ .

11. After dinner they crowded by the fire telling and listening to
🔔 < ☼ ☞ ↑ ⇨ 🔔
__________ .

Color the pumpkins and the pumpkin pie.

Our Thanksgiving Celebration

Pretend that you have a pen pal in England. On a separate piece of paper, write a letter to your pen pal, telling about your family's Thanksgiving celebration. After you and your parent make corrections, copy it onto this page.

Learning about Pumpkins

Pumpkin is still an important part of the American Thanksgiving feast. The pumpkin plant is native to North America. These plants are members of the gourd family. They grow on vines that produce green **leaves**, large yellow-orange **flowers**, thin green **tendrils**, and pumpkins, which is the fruit of the pumpkin vine. The outside of the pumpkin is called the **shell**. The shell has two parts: the thin outer rind (or skin) and the thick **pulp**. At the center of the pumpkin is a cavity filled with **seeds** and slimy fibrous strands. People eat both the pulp and the seeds. The pulp has vitamins, minerals, fiber, and antioxidants. Pumpkin pulp makes tasty pie, soup, muffins, cookies, and bread. The seeds are high in manganese, magnesium, and phosphorus, and they taste great.

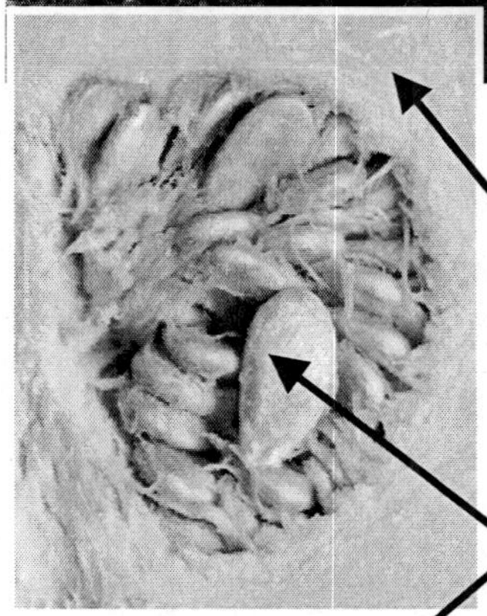

Use the descriptions above to label the parts of a pumpkin. They are printed in ***bold****.*

Early Presidents Proclaim Days of Thanksgiving

Early in our history as a nation, presidents declared national days of Thanksgiving. George Washington did so in 1789 and 1795, John Adams in 1798 and 1799, and James Madison twice in 1815.

Many of the Founding Fathers of the United States showed great respect for God and for His role in our lives. In the proclamation on these two pages, each pronoun that refers to God has been underlined. In addition to the title of Almighty God, there are four other nouns that refer to God. Circle **Almighty God** *and each of those other* **nouns**. *A key to being thankful is recognizing our blessings. Underline the words* **thank** *and* **bless** *and every other word that has* **thank** *or* **bless** *as its* **root word**. *Then, read the proclamation again.*

George Washington's 1789 Thanksgiving Proclamation

Whereas it is the duty of all nations to acknowledge the providence of Almighty God, to obey **His** will, to be grateful for **His** benefits, and humbly to implore **His** protection and favor; and Whereas both Houses of Congress have, by their joint committee, requested me "to recommend to the people of the United States a day of public thanksgiving and prayer, to be observed by acknowledging with

This 1866 print from the Library of Congress was engraved by John C. McRae and is entitled The Prayer at Valley Forge. It is based on a painting by H. Brueckner.

grateful hearts the many and signal favors of Almighty God, especially by affording them an opportunity peaceably to establish a form of government for their safety and happiness."

Now, therefore I do recommend and assign Thursday, the 26th day of November next, to be devoted by the people of these States to the service of that great and glorious Being who is the beneficent Author of all the good that was, that is, or that will be; that we may then all unite in rendering unto **Him** our sincere and humble thanks for **His** kind care and protection of the people of this country previous to their becoming a nation; for the signal and manifold mercies and the favorable interpositions of **His** providence in the course and conclusion of the late war; for the great degree of tranquility, union, and plenty which we have since enjoyed; for the peaceable and rational manner in which we have been enabled to establish constitutions of government for our safety and happiness, and particularly the national one now lately instituted for the civil and religious liberty with which we are blessed, and the means we have of acquiring and diffusing useful knowledge; and, in general, for all the great and various favors which **He** has been pleased to confer upon us.

And also that we may then unite in most humbly offering our prayers and supplications to the great Lord and Ruler of Nations and beseech **Him** to pardon our national and other transgressions; to enable us all, whether in public or private stations, to perform our several and relative duties properly and punctually; to render our National Government a blessing to all the people by constantly being a Government of wise, just, and constitutional laws, discreetly and faithfully executed and obeyed; to protect and guide all sovereigns and nations (especially such as have shown kindness to us), and to bless them with good governments, peace, and concord; to promote the knowledge and practice of true religion and virtue, and the increase of science among them and us; and, generally to grant unto all mankind such a degree of temporal prosperity as **He** alone knows to be best.

Given under my hand, at the city of New York, the 3d day of October, A.D. 1789.

Thanksgiving Nouns

A noun is a person, place, or thing. Here is a list of Thanksgiving nouns.
Can you fit them into the puzzle below?

CRANBERRIES RELATIVES TURKEY PRAYER
AUTUMN GRANDPARENTS BLESSINGS DINNER HOLIDAY
PUMPKIN GOD FAMILY

T
H
A
N
K
S
G
I
V
I
N
G

A Cornucopia of Blessings

Samuel McIntire was an architect and a woodcarver who lived from 1757 to 1811. He designed houses for wealthy residents of Salem, Massachusetts. He also carved decorations for doors, mantels, and furniture. He helped make designs of American eagles and cornucopias popular in American culture. The cornucopia is still a symbol of Thanksgiving.

Color the cornucopia and the blessings of the harvest.

Lydia Maria Child Writes a Thanksgiving Favorite

Lydia Maria Child

Lydia Maria Francis was born in 1802 in Medford, Massachusetts. Medford is the fourth oldest English settlement in the United States and one of the towns Paul Revere rode through when he announced that the British were coming during the American Revolution. Maria was taught at home, at a dame school, and at a women's seminary.

When Maria grew up, she wrote the novel *Hobomok* and founded a children's magazine called *Juvenile Miscellany*. She later married David Lee Child and continued to write. One of the books she wrote was *The Frugal Housewife*, an advice book for women. David and Maria worked in the abolitionist movement. Before the Civil War, abolitionists worked to free African American slaves. Lydia Maria Child also worked to help American women receive the right to vote.

In 1844, Lydia Maria Child published *Flowers for Children*, which included "A Boy's Thanksgiving Day." It has become America's most famous Thanksgiving song.

"A Boy's Thanksgiving Day" is printed on the following page.
Around the page are several words from the poem.
Find those words in the puzzle.

Grandfather's · play · Thanksgiving · gate · drifted

house · white · Day · over · Grandmother's · nose · toes · go

A Boy's Thanksgiving Day

Over the river and through the wood,
To Grandfather's house we go.
The horse knows the way to carry the sleigh
Through the white and drifted snow.

Over the river and through the wood —
Oh, how the wind does blow!
It stings the toes and bites the nose,
As over the ground we go.

Over the river and through the wood,
To have a first-rate play.
Hear the bells ring, "Ting-a-ling-ding!"
Hurrah for Thanksgiving Day!

Over the river and through the wood
Trot fast, my dapple-gray!
Spring over the ground, like a hunting hound!
For this is Thanksgiving Day.

Over the river and through the wood,
And straight through the barn yard gate.
We seem to go extremely slow,
It is so hard to wait!

Over the river and through the wood —
Now Grandmother's cap I spy!
Hurrah for the fun! Is the pudding done?
Hurrah for the pumpkin pie!

G	P	T	O	E	S	D	A
R	U	H	U	R	R	A	H
A	M	A	B	B	B	Y	O
N	P	N	T	R	O	T	U
D	K	K	C	C	C	H	S
M	I	S	N	O	W	O	E
O	N	G	A	T	E	U	D
T	R	I	V	E	R	N	E
H	O	V	E	R	F	D	F
E	G	I	W	H	I	T	E
R	C	N	O	S	E	H	H
S	A	G	O	I	F	I	F
G	P	U	D	D	I	N	G
R	J	L	J	P	J	L	J
A	B	E	L	L	S	K	K
N	A	L	L	L	L	L	L
D	R	I	F	T	E	D	S
F	N	M	M	M	M	M	T
A	N	P	L	A	Y	N	I
T	Q	A	W	Q	A	W	N
H	O	R	S	E	H	H	G
E	V	B	N	V	B	N	S
R	C	V	B	C	V	B	C
S	L	E	I	G	H	Y	U
Q	W	E	R	T	Y	U	I

Hurrah · bells · hound · pudding · cap · pumpkin · trot · barn

stings · horse · sleigh · snow · wood · river

Thankful Words

The English language has many words we can use to express thanksgiving for our blessings. Can you find these in the puzzle below?

APPRECIATE **APPRECIATED** **APPRECIATION** **APPRECIATIVE**

GRATEFUL **GRATEFULNESS** **GRATITUDE**

THANK **THANKFUL** **THANKFULNESS** **THANKS** **THANKSGIVING**

						Q	P	M	M	T	H	A	N	K	F	U	L
						A	O	N	N	H	Q	W	A	S	D	F	G
						Z	I	B	B	A	L	K	P	A	S	D	F
						W	T	H	A	N	K	S	P	Q	W	E	R
						S	U	V	V	K	P	O	R	U	Y	T	R
G	R	A	T	E	F	U	L	N	E	S	S	L	E	K	J	H	T
A	B	P	A	S	Z	W	T	C	C	G	I	U	C	L	K	J	H
C	D	P	C	A	P	P	R	E	C	I	A	T	I	O	N	U	A
E	F	R	E	T	X	E	T	L	X	V	L	K	A	J	H	G	N
G	G	E	G	V	C	R	R	K	Z	I	L	K	T	H	A	N	K
H	H	C	I	X	V	T	E	J	P	N	A	S	I	D	G	F	T
J	I	I	K	Z	B	Y	W	H	O	G	Q	N	V	P	R	Y	Y
G	R	A	T	E	F	U	L	G	I	L	W	H	E	L	A	G	L
L	K	T	L	A	N	U	L	F	G	K	E	Y	Q	M	T	V	Q
N	M	E	N	D	B	I	G	R	A	T	I	T	U	D	E	F	A
P	O	T	P	C	M	O	J	S	T	H	T	G	Z	K	T	R	Z
R	Q	A	P	P	R	E	C	I	A	T	E	D	W	J	U	T	W
S	R	V	R	W	Q	P	H	A	R	F	Y	G	S	I	D	Y	S
T	H	A	N	K	F	U	L	N	E	S	S	B	X	U	E	U	X

Overflowing with Thanksgiving

Read Colossians 2:6-7. Copy it on the lines below and then complete the sentences at the bottom of the page.

Colossians 2:6-7

____

____

____

____

____

____

I appreciate ____.

I feel appreciated when ______________________________________.

I like to show appreciation by __________________________________.

I feel appreciative for _______________________________________.

I am grateful for ____.

I overflow with gratefulness when ______________________________.

I feel gratitude when ____.

I would like to thank ____.

I feel thankful for ____.

I am filled with thankfulness when _____________________________.

I would like to say thanks to ___________________________________.

I like Thanksgiving because ____________________________________.

Lesson 9 – History, Magazines, Drawing, Letter Writing

Thanksgiving Becomes an Official National Holiday

Some of the words in this lesson are printed incorrectly. Each incorrect word rhymes with the word that should have been used. Here is a list of the correct words. Cross out each incorrect word and replace it with the correct one. When you have finished filling in the blanks, read the lesson again.

EACH YEAR CELEBRATE LAST DECLARE WEST FIRST HALE NEW TRADITION

Though Thanksgiving was not a national holiday during the early 1800s, Americans continued to celebrate the feast, mainly in **MOO** ________ England. There each state declared an annual Thanksgiving, usually in November. As New Englanders moved **GUEST** __________, they carried the Thanksgiving **PHYSICIAN** ______________ with them. Other states began to **DECORATE** _____________ it, too. The Southern states were the last to adopt the practice that they at **BURST** ____________ considered a "Yankee" holiday.

President Abraham Lincoln

Each November from 1846 to 1863, Sarah Josepha **MAIL** ____________, editor of the *Godey's Lady's Book,* wrote editorials urging the United States government to **BEWARE** _______________ Thanksgiving a national holiday. In 1863 Abraham Lincoln declared the **FAST** _____________ Thursday in November to be Thanksgiving Day. Afterwards, **PEACH** ___________ President followed his example. Between 1863 and 1938, the last Thursday in November was Thanksgiving each **PIER** ___________ except for two.

Thanksgiving in Magazines

Louis Antoine Godey co-founded *Lady's Book* in 1830 in Philadelphia, Pennsylvania. It was the first American magazine entirely devoted to articles of special interest to women. He later became its only owner and it became *Godey's Lady's Book*. The magazine published pieces by many famous American writers, including Nathaniel Hawthore, Henry Wadsworth Longfellow, and Harriet Beecher Stowe. In 1837, Sarah Josepha Hale became its editor.

Hale encouraged people to think about an annual Thanksgiving holiday. Today's editors of ladies' magazines continue to help people think about and prepare for Thanksgiving.

Pretend you are a magazine editor. On a separate sheet of paper, make a list of Thanksgiving articles you would include in your magazine. Create intriguing titles for them. Copy your article ideas below. Design the cover for your November issue in the frame.

1. Subject of article: ____________________

   ____

   Title: ____________________

   ____

2. Subject of article: ____________________

   ____

   Title: ____________________

   ____

3. Subject of article: ____________________

   ____

   Title: ____________________

   ____

4. Subject of article: ____________________

   ____

   Title: ____________________

   ____

A Civil War Thanksgiving

On Thursday, November 28, 1861, some Union soldiers celebrated Thanksgiving in camp. Artist Alfred Rudolph Waud sketched this picture of their celebration. The sketch was drawn in pencil on tan paper. The smoke was added with an artist's medium known as Chinese white. The original sketch is preserved in the Library of Congress. Copy the entire sketch or parts of it in the frame below.

A Soldier's Letter Home

Pretend you are one of the Union soldiers in the sketch.
On a separate piece of paper, write a letter home telling about your Thanksgiving Day.
After you and your parent make corrections, copy it onto this page.

President Abraham Lincoln visits the troops at Antietam.

Lesson 10 — Art, Creative Writing, Sports, Puzzle

Thanksgiving During the Late 1800s

This lithograph is from the Library of Congress. Currier and Ives published it in New York in 1867. The title is "Home to Thanksgiving." Nathaniel Currier founded a lithograph business in the 1830s in New York City. He later made one of his employees, James Merritt Ives, his partner. Currier died in 1888 and Ives in 1895. The firm published lithographs of everyday life and of major disasters until 1907. Look carefully at the detail in the picture. On a separate piece of paper, write a description of it. After you and your parent make corrections, copy your description onto this page and page 39.

____

____

____

____

Our Thanksgiving Scene

Think of the place that you celebrate Thanksgiving. On a separate piece of paper, describe what that place looks like on Thanksgiving Day. After you and your parent make corrections, copy it onto this page.

Thanksgiving Football

Artist's depiction of a Yale-Princeton game in late 1800s.

Princeton, **Yale**, **Harvard**, and **Columbia** Universities formed the Intercollegiate **Football** Association in 1874. The association held its first **Thanksgiving Day** championship game in New York City in 1876. The first **professional** football **game** took place in 1895. Today both the Detroit **Lions** and the Dallas **Cowboys** play games on Thanksgiving Day.

Find the underlined words above in the puzzle below.

F	L	C	T	R	T	H	A	N	K	S	G	I	V	I	N	G	D	A	Y
P	R	O	F	E	S	S	I	O	N	A	L	H	H	A	R	V	A	R	D
O	A	L	I	V	T	O	N	Q	W	E	I	I	A	S	D	F	G	H	J
O	S	U	O	A	Y	Y	A	L	R	C	O	W	B	O	Y	S	I	G	P
T	O	M	N	R	A	C	E	T	O	N	N	V	A	R	D	H	A	A	P
B	C	B	H	D	L	C	O	W	Q	W	S	B	O	Y	S	D	F	M	R
P	R	I	N	C	E	T	O	N	M	N	B	V	C	X	S	D	F	E	I
A	I	A	A	P	R	I	N	C	E	F	F	O	O	T	B	A	L	L	N

Photograph of Harvard-Yale football game on November 25, 1911. Photo from the Library of Congress.

Harvard Football Team from late 1800s.

Yale Football Team from late 1800s.

Princeton Football Team from late 1800s.

Edward Penfield created this cover for the November 1894 issue of Harper's Magazine. *The man is sporting a Yale sweater and a Yale vs. Harvard football poster is in the background. Courtesy of the Library of Congress.*

Lesson 11 — History, Bible Study, Creative Writing, Puzzle

Room for All at Our Table of Thanksgiving

Everyone in the world is an immigrant or the descendant of an immigrant. First, God sent Adam and Eve out of the Garden of Eden and later He scattered many people at the Tower of Babel. In Acts 17:26 Paul told people in Athens, Greece, that God "...made from one, every nation of mankind to live on all the face of the earth, having determined their appointed times, and the boundaries of their habitation..."

James, John, Joseph, and Fletcher Harper were publishers during the 1800s. Harper and Brothers began publishing magazines, such as *Harper's New Monthly*

This illustration from the November 20, 1869 issue of Harper's Weekly *depicts men, women, and children from many nations. Uncle Sam is carving a turkey. The centerpiece states "Self-Government; Universal Suffrage." The artist is Thomas Nast, whose drawing of Santa Claus has been a major influence on the American celebration of Christmas.*

This illustration from the November 29, 1884 issue of Harper's Weekly *is entitled, "Castle Garden — Their First Thanksgiving Dinner." Castle Garden was the first stop for immigrants coming into New York City before Ellis Island was built in 1892. Courtesy of the Library of Congress.*

Magazine (1850, pictured on page 41), *Harper's Weekly* (1857), and *Harper's Bazar* (1867, William Randolph Hearst later bought this periodical and added another "a" to Bazar). *Harper's Weekly* helped readers consider the plight of immigrants. Note the illustrations on these two pages. Today many Americans reach out to homeless people and others in need on Thanksgiving Day by providing them with a special Thanksgiving meal.

Copy Matthew 25:35.

This photograph from the Library of Congress is entitled,
"The Beggar Boy's Thanksgiving."
It was published around 1871.

On a separate piece of paper, write a short story about one of the pictures in lesson 11. After you and your parent make corrections, copy it onto this page.

Love God and Love Your Neighbor

But when the Pharisees heard that He
had put the Sadducees to silence,
they gathered themselves together. And one of them,
a lawyer, asked Him a question, testing Him,
"**Teacher**, which is the **great** commandment in the Law?"
And He said to him,
"'You shall **love** the Lord your God with all your **heart**,
and with all your **soul**, and with all your **mind**.'
This is the great and **foremost** **commandment**.
The second is like it,
'You shall love your **neighbor** as **yourself**.'
On these two commandments depend
the whole Law and the Prophets."
Matthew 22:34-40

Find the underlined words in the puzzle below.

T	E	A	C	H	E	R	H	A	P	P	Y	A	H	P	O	P	U	Y	Y
T	H	A	N	K	S	G	I	V	I	N	G	N	E	I	G	H	B	O	R
G	G	M	A	T	T	H	E	W	L	U	K	E	A	L	J	I	F	U	T
E	R	I	O	S	T	I	M	O	T	H	Y	I	R	K	A	L	G	R	R
N	E	S	C	O	M	M	A	N	D	M	E	N	T	J	M	L	H	S	E
E	A	E	D	U	Q	W	E	R	T	I	I	U	Y	H	E	I	J	E	W
S	T	X	U	L	O	V	E	L	K	N	J	H	G	G	S	P	K	L	A
E	P	H	E	S	I	A	N	S	U	D	P	O	I	F	V	I	L	F	S
R	O	M	A	N	S	Z	X	C	V	B	F	O	R	E	M	O	S	T	D

Lesson 12 — History, Creative Writing, Costumes

Thanksgiving in the Early 1900s

This photograph from the Library of Congress is entitled, "Blake school Thanksgiving dinner to school officials." It is dated November 25, 1925.

Thanksgiving is usually thought of as a family holiday, but some people celebrate in large groups. Sometimes this large dinner is in addition to the family gathering, and sometimes people are not able to be with their families on Thanksgiving. Look at the photograph at left. Notice that the adults are sitting in chairs and the children are sitting on benches. Does your family have special places for the children to sit? At my grandparents' house, I sat at a little wooden children's table until it was needed by younger children. Then I moved up to a kitchen counter. It was many years before I got to sit at the tables with the adults. I enjoy remembering all the different places I got to sit.

Holiday activities vary from one family to another and from one region of the country to another.

This photograph from the Library of Congress is entitled, "Dogsled crossing bay on Thanksgiving Day." The photograph was taken in Alaska in the early 1900s.

Sometimes they vary because of climate. Notice the picture at the bottom of page 46. This person could dogsled on Thanksgiving Day because he was in Alaska. In the early 1900s, farmers in the southern states killed hogs on Thanksgiving Day because the weather was cold and the meat would not spoil.

Look at the photo to the right. The man in the center is holding a turkey upside down by its feet. He probably didn't kill hogs or go dogsledding on Thanksgiving Day!

This photograph from the Library of Congress is entitled, "Thanksgiving, 1919."

Imagine that the man holding the turkey is your father, the lady on the right in a striped skirt is your mother, and the little girl is your sister. On a separate piece of paper, write a paragraph about what your family is doing on Thanksgiving Day. After you and your parent make corrections, copy it onto this page.

Pilgrim Costumes

The "Pilgrims" on this page are actually wearing clothing like Boston Puritans wore after 1632. However, these costumes have become symbols of the Plymouth Pilgrims of 1620. Look at the picture on page 49. Notice that this kind of costume had already become symbolic of the Pilgrims by the early 1900s. Though Pilgrims are often pictured wearing only black and white, they actually had no restrictions against wearing colors. They had dyes of red, green, beige, burgundy, blue, violet, and brown, in addition to black. Use a variety of these colors to color these Pilgrims' clothes, but color each clothing item in only one solid color.

This photograph from the George Grantham Bain Collection in the Library of Congress is entitled, "School Children's Thanksgiving Games." It is dated November 27, 1911. On a separate piece of paper, write a description of the scene. After you and your parent make corrections, copy it onto this page.

Lesson 13 — History, Science

The Thanksgiving Turkey

Turkeys have long been associated with Thanksgiving. In 1942, Norman Rockwell painted a series of pictures known as the Four Freedoms. *Freedom from Want* depicts a family sitting around a dinner table. At the head of the table stand a grandmother and grandfather admiring a platter of turkey. Grandma Moses, another famous American artist, created the *Thanksgiving Turkey* painting in 1943.

The most traditional main course for the American Thanksgiving Day is certainly turkey. In fact, the National Turkey Federation estimates that 46 million turkeys are eaten for Thanksgiving and another 22 million are eaten for Christmas!

Minnesota raises more turkeys than any other state. North Carolina, Arkansas, Missouri, Virginia, Indiana, and California are also major turkey producing states. American turkey farmers export turkeys to Mexico, China, Russia, Canada, and other countries.

This photograph from the Library of Congress is entitled, "Thanksgiving — taking home turkeys from raffle." It is dated November 22, 1912.

A large group of turkeys is a flock, a male is a tom, a female is a hen, and a baby is a poult.

Benjamin Franklin had so much respect for turkeys that he praised them in a letter to his daughter. He told her it would make a better

This photograph from the Library of Congress is from the early 1900s.

national symbol than the eagle. The turkey has become a symbol of Thanksgiving. It has been honored in other ways, too. Turkey, Texas, has a population of about 425 residents. Turkey, North Carolina, has about 300

Today most families buy their Thanksgiving turkey from a grocery store, but at one time, killing, plucking, and cooking the turkey were part of the preparations for Thanksgiving Day.

Write funny captions under these turkey and Pilgrim cartoons.

Color this scene with wild turkeys.

Both of these photographs from the Library of Congress bear the same title: "Thanksgiving, 1919."

The Fourth Thursday of November

President Roosevelt

In 1939, President Franklin Roosevelt declared Thanksgiving to be the next to last Thursday in November. Merchants had asked him to change the date so that the Christmas shopping season would be longer. The date change caused an uproar and some people began to call the holiday "Franksgiving." President Roosevelt admitted his mistake, and in 1941 he signed a bill establishing the fourth Thursday in November as the official Thanksgiving Day for the United States.

Turkeys and Presidents

Inside these elaborate crates are two turkeys received by President Harding in 1921. The one on the left was a gift from Cuero, Texas; the one on the right came from H.W. Mason of Crystal Springs, Mississippi. Courtesy of the Library of Congress.

Every year the President of the United States receives turkeys as gifts. Every modern president hosts a ceremony where he pardons one of his gift turkeys before Thanksgiving Day. Actually he pardons two, since another turkey is chosen as an alternate in case the first turkey cannot perform his duties at the ceremony. For many years the turkeys went to Frying Pan Park, a petting zoo in Virginia. From 2005 to 2009, the birds were sent to Disneyland or Walt Disney World. In 2010 they went to Mount Vernon.

Since 2003, the White House has let the public vote on naming these turkeys. Use the secret code on page 55 to find out some of the winning names. Fill in the signs with names you would choose.

1 = A   2 = B   3 = C   4 = D
5 = E   6 = F   7 =G   8 = H   9 = I
10 = J   11 = K   12 = L   13 = M
14 = N   15 = O   16 = P   17 = Q
18 = R   19 = S   20 = T   21 = U
22 = V   23 = W   24 = X
25 = Y   26 = Z

19 20 1 18 19 ____________ and 19 20 18 9 16 5 19 ________________

2 9 19 3 21 9 20 ________________ and 7 18 1 22 25 ______________

13 1 18 19 8 13 1 12 12 15 23 ____________________ and 25 1 13 ________

6 12 25 5 18 ________________ and 6 18 25 5 18 ________________

Parades on Thanksgiving Day

Several major cities host Thanksgiving Day parades, including Chicago, Detroit, Houston, and Philadelphia. The most famous parade is in New York City. In 1924, Macy's department store employees held their first Thanksgiving Day parade. Its success caused Macy's to make the parade an annual event. In 1927, the parade introduced its first giant helium-filled balloon, Felix the Cat. The parade has continued every year except 1942-1944, when Macy's donated the rubber from its balloons to help American forces in World War II. In the 1930s, people started listening to the parade on radio and in 1945 it was shown for the first time on television.

Children looking at Christmas toys through the window of New York City's Macy's department store. This Library of Congress photograph was taken in the early 1900s.

How God Gives Us Our Thanksgiving Dinner

A modern Thanksgiving celebration includes many blessings from God. How does God give us these wonderful blessings? Let's look at the Creation week and see!

Before reading the rest of this lesson, read Genesis chapter 1 and Genesis 2:1-3.

On the **first day** of Creation, God made light. Light lets us see how to prepare the meal and lets us see our loved ones around the table. The light God made on day one gives us energy. We use lots of energy to cook the great meal and to travel to the site of our Thanksgiving celebration.

On the **second day**, God made the sky. Water from the sky comes down as rain. Rain is necessary for our food to grow.

On the **third day** of creation, God made the dry ground appear. That's why we have a place for fruits and vegetables to grow. God put nutrients in the soil to nourish the plants that nourish us. On the the third day, He put the water in special places. We use that water to cook our food, to make tea, and to wash all those Thanksgiving dishes. God also created many different kinds of plants on day three. Our Thanksgiving dinner might include:

- Cranberries, green beans, pumpkins, and squashes that grow on vines;
- tea from Asia;
- sugar cane from tropical regions to sweeten;

- sweet potatoes and onions that grow underground (onions go in the stuffing);
- stalks of wheat for rolls and pie crust; and
- stalks of corn for our cornbread.

On **the fourth day**, God created the sun to shine on plants and to make them grow.

On the **fifth day** of creation, God made birds, including turkeys. Some families eat wild turkeys for Thanksgiving. Wild turkeys eat foods that God created, like insects, grasses, acorns, seeds, and fruits. Other families eat tame turkeys that farmers raise. God also made the chicken eggs that go in our stuffing and in our pumpkin pies and other desserts.

On the **sixth day**, God made people in His image. He made people who want to thank Him for His blessings. Because we are made in His image, we can figure out how to take those things He has made and make a yummy Thanksgiving dinner.

On the seventh day, God rested. He blesses us with rest, too. Lots of folks need rest after Thanksgiving dinner. Just ask your mother!

Thank God for the blessings of His creation.

Remembering...

Thanksgiving is a time to remember our blessings. As you complete the creative writing on page 60, you will remember your blessings. On this page, you will remember what you have learned in your study of Thanksgiving. Fill in the blanks of the statements below. Find a place for each answer in the puzzle on page 59 . Fill in the puzzle and color the picture.

1. William ____________ served as governor of the Plymouth Colony.
2. Abraham ____________ made Thanksgiving an official ____________.
3. The name of the Pilgrims' ship was the ____________.
4. Architect Samuel McIntire helped make the ____________________ design popular in America.
5. William ____________________ led the Separatists.
6. God wants us to be ________________ for our blessings.
7. Chief ____________________ joined the Pilgrims in their harvest celebration of 1621.
8. A Scripture often associated with Thanksgiving is __________ 100.
9. A popular Thanksgiving hymn is "We ___________ Together."
10. The Pilgrims sailed from Plymouth, ______________.
11. "The Boy's Thanksgiving Day" was written by Lydia Maria ____________.
12. President ____________ set Thanksgiving Day as the fourth Thursday of November.
13. ____________ taught the Pilgrims how to plant corn.
14. Families in America have passed down different Thanksgiving _________________.
15. America has welcomed many _________________________ from foreign lands.
16. George _______________________ made a Thanksgiving proclamation in 1789.
17. The Pilgrims sailed to America and settled at what is now _________________, __________________________.
18. In the autumn, farmers gather in the _______________ God has helped them grow.
19. The first settlers at Plymouth, Massachusetts are called ____________________.

... and Looking Ahead ...

Do the activity on page 60.

... To Future Generations

Think about a future Thanksgiving many years from now. Imagine that you are the man on the right or the lady in the middle and that you and your loved ones are celebrating Thanksgiving Day. You want to tell your loved ones about the history of Thanksgiving and about how the Lord has blessed you all your life. On a separate piece of paper, write down what you would say. After you and your parent make corrections, copy it onto this page.

Fun with Thanksgiving Trivia

To learn and remember some Thanksgiving trivia, fill in the blanks below with words from this list.

CAR CRANBURY PILGRIM DETROIT DRESSING
HOSTS GROWN MAJOR CAPITAL FRIED

1. A town in New Jersey is named (proper noun with two R's) ________________.
2. A township in Missouri is named (proper noun with two I's) ________________.
3. __________ (proper noun with two T's) has an annual Christmas parade and its NFL team always plays on Thanksgiving Day.
4. Some families in the south eat (adjective) __________ turkey on Thanksgiving Day.
5. According to the Bureau of Transportation Statistics, of people who travel a long distance over the Thanksgiving weekend, 91 percent travel by (object of a preposition) ____________.
6. According to the University of Illinois, 90 percent of the pumpkins (verb) ________ in the United States are grown within a 90-mile radius of Peoria, Illinois. Other major pumpkin-producing states are California, Ohio, and Pennsylvania.
7. The main sweet potato-producing state is North Carolina. Other (adjective) ____________ producers are California, Mississippi, and Louisiana.
8. Southerners make a dish that is similar to stuffing, but it is not cooked inside the turkey. That dish is (a noun that can also be verb) ____________.
9. Morton, Illinois, claims to be the Pumpkin (a noun with two A's) __________ of the World.
10. Vardaman, Mississippi, (verb) __________ an annual Sweet Potato Festival.

Thanksgiving Crafts

Thanksgiving Place Cards

Make place cards for your family's Thanksgiving dinner. Here's how:

Supplies Needed:

- ✓ 3″ x 5″ index cards
- ✓ Pencil
- ✓ Fine-tip pens or colored pencils

Directions:

1. Fold blank index cards in half to make a 3 x 2 ½ inch rectangle.
2. Draw a Pilgrim hat on each card.
3. Letter Psalm 106:1 at the top of each card.
4. Write each guest's name on the hat.

Service Idea

Make similar cards (see right) and take them to a nursing home. You can use stickers to decorate them.

Thanksgiving Recipe Cards

Decorate blank index cards with small Thanksgiving designs. Simply write A Thanksgiving Favorite at the top and draw a pretty Thanksgiving design in one of the top corners. Design ideas are included on pages 72-73.

Supplies Needed:

- ✓ 3″ x 5″ index cards
- ✓ Pencil
- ✓ Fine-tip pens or colored pencils

Options:

1. Make a set to give as a thank you gift to your Thanksgiving hostess, your mother, or another friend or relative.
2. Make a set for yourself. Ask your relatives to write their favorite Thanksgiving recipes on them so you will have them when it's your turn to make the dinner sometime in the future.
3. Use stickers instead of drawing pictures.

Thanksgiving Cards

Make cards to use as Thanksgiving greetings, invitations, or thank you notes.

Supplies Needed:

- ✓ 8 ½″ by 11″ heavy white or colored paper
- ✓ Pencil
- ✓ Fine-tip pens or colored pencils
- ✓ Letter or legal size envelopes

Directions:

If you are using letter-size envelopes, cut paper into 7″ x 6 ¼″ rectangles. Fold in half to make 3 ½″ x 6 ¼″ cards. If you are using legal-size envelopes, cut paper into 8″ x 9 ¼″ rectangles. Fold in half to make 4″ x 9 ¼″ cards. Add words and Thanksgiving designs. Design ideas are included on pages 72-73.

A Hand Print Turkey

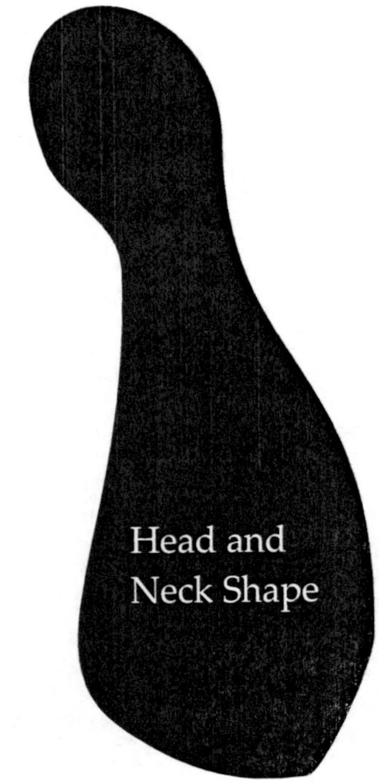

Make a hand print turkey to put on your door.

Supplies Needed:

- ✓ White poster board
- ✓ Construction paper in yellow, gold, orange, red, and brown
- ✓ Pencil
- ✓ Scissors
- ✓ Two yellow, brown, or gold pipe cleaners (Construction paper can be used instead.)
- ✓ Glue stick

Directions:

Cut a gold oval about 12-14 inches across and 16 inches high for the body. Cut a brown shape about 16 inches tall for the head and neck. Cut red wattle shape about four inches long. Cut a yellow triangle about 1 ½ inches tall for the beak. Trace some children's hand prints on every color of the construction paper. Make feet out of pipe cleaners. Write a greeting at the top of the poster board. Glue pieces as shown in the diagram below.

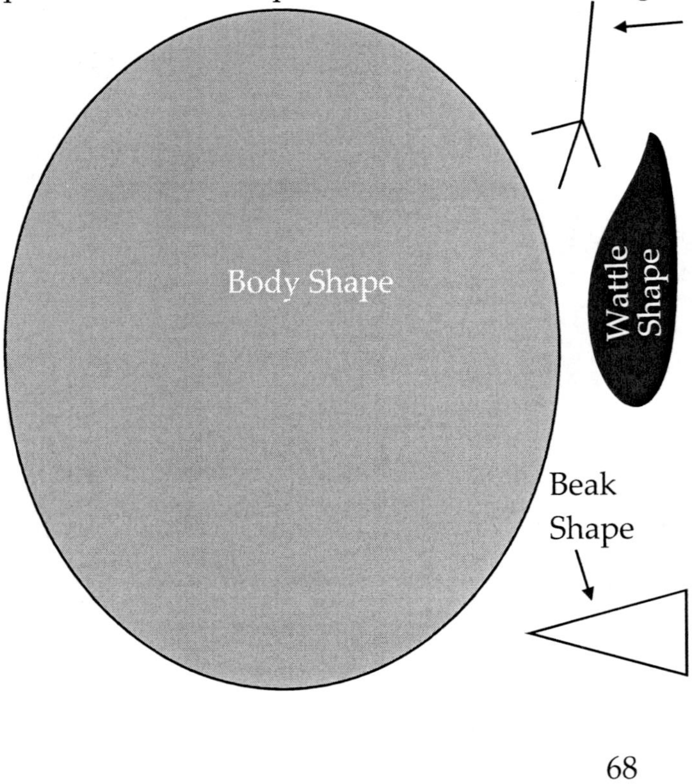

Fall Creation Arrangement

Go for a walk on an autumn day and find seed pods, colorful leaves, pine cones, and other things. Be careful to stay away from poison ivy and other plants that may hurt you. Lay your treasures on a pretty tray or in a basket to make a centerpiece for your Thanksgiving table. If you have small pumpkins, apples, or unshelled nuts, you can place those in your arrangement, too.

A Cookie and Candy Turkey

We love to make these fun Thanksgiving turkey desserts. It's one of our Thanksgiving traditions. Here's how:

Mom, Grandmother, and Daniel with our turkeys

Purchase the following ingredients:

- ✓ Graham crackers or thin cookie for the base
- ✓ Candy corn for the turkey's head
- ✓ Cream drop candies or other cone-shaped candy for turkey's body (cream drops are cone-shaped with white cream centers and a chocolate coating)
- ✓ Cookies with scalloped edges for the turkey's tail
- ✓ Canned frosting (you can make your own, if you prefer; that's what we do)

Assemble your turkeys like this:

Break rectangle graham crackers in half to make square bases for the turkeys. Lay a creme drop on its side to make the turkey's body. Attach it to the graham cracker with frosting. Attach a butter cookie to the flat side of the creme drop for the turkey's tail. Attach a piece of candy corn to the point of the creme drop for the turkey's head. Make candy and cookie turkeys for a great Thanksgiving evening snack or as a special treat for elderly neighbors.

Caution:
Be careful to substitute other ingredients if your children or guests are allergic to any ingredients in these processed foods.

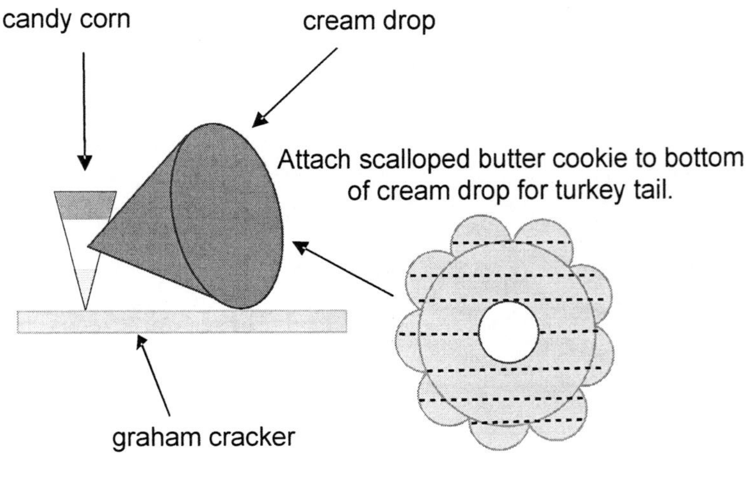

An Heirloom Tablecloth

Make a cherished family heirloom. Our family made one several years ago and now we have the handprints and signatures of three family members who have left us for eternity. We are so thankful that we took some extra time one Thanksgiving and made this cherished possession! Here's how you can make one, too!

A few days before Thanksgiving, gather these supplies:

- ✓ Non-toxic fabric paints in three fall colors
- ✓ A white, yellow, or beige tablecloth or flat sheet
- ✓ Black fabric marker
- ✓ Old newspapers
- ✓ Paper plates

On Thanksgiving morning before guests arrive:

1. Cover a table thickly with newspapers to protect it from paint and marker.
2. Cover newspapers with tablecloth or sheet.
3. Lay out paint, paper plates, and markers.

When guests arrive:

Spread a thin layer of each paint color onto paper plates. Have each family member make one or two hand prints. Have each guest sign his name under his hand print(s). With the black marker, add an eye, a beak, and a wattle to each "turkey."

Traditional Designs for Thanksgiving Projects

You can use these designs for crafts on pages 66-67 or let them spark your own creative ideas for Thanksgiving projects. You may draw from them or trace them for any non-commercial use. You may photocopy pages 72 and 73.

Some Fun Designs for Thanksgiving Projects

You can use these designs for crafts on pages 66-67 or let them spark your own creative ideas for Thanksgiving projects. You may draw from them or trace them for any non-commercial use. You may photocopy pages 72 and 73.

Thanksgiving Scrapbook

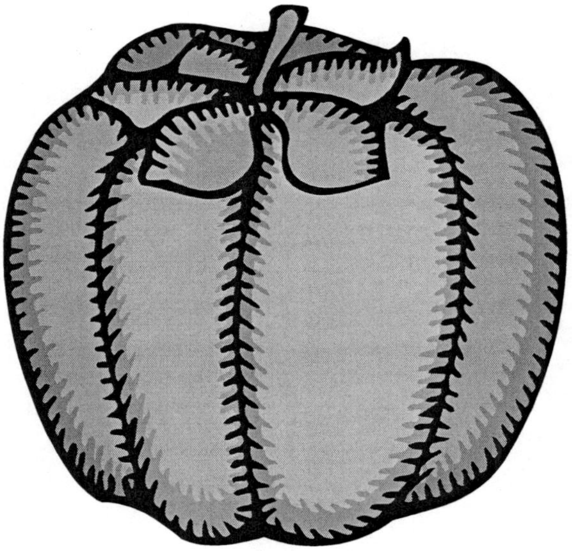

Scrapbook Ideas

This section is a place for you to keep memories of your family's Thanksgiving celebration. Here are some ideas of things you might include in your scrapbook. The paper is acid-free.

Autographs of your family, relatives, and friends who spend Thanksgiving with you.
Outlines of their hands.
Portraits you have drawn of your family, relatives, and friends.
Family recipes.
Thanksgiving pictures from magazines (be sure to get an adult's permission first).
A written account of Thanksgiving Day.
Memorabilia from any outings you go on during Thanksgiving weekend.
Tickets from any events you attend.
Tickets from any public transportation you take.
A place card from the Thanksgiving table.
A few photographs (usually families keep photograph albums for everyone, but your family may be able to share a few duplicates with you).
Thanksgiving artwork created by you, your relatives, and friends.
Any Thanksgiving cards or invitations you receive.
A long list of your blessings!

Happy Scrapbooking!

My Thanksgiving Blessings

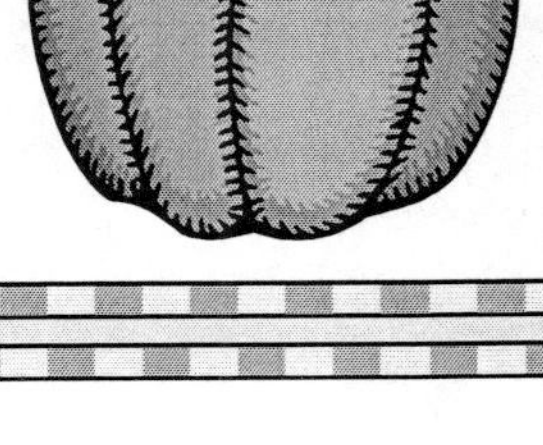

My Thanksgiving Blessings

My Thanksgiving Blessings

My Thanksgiving Blessings

My Thanksgiving Blessings

My Thanksgiving Blessings

My Thanksgiving Blessings

My Thanksgiving Blessings

My Thanksgiving Blessings

My Thanksgiving Blessings

My Thanksgiving Blessings

My Thanksgiving Blessings

Answer Key

Lesson 1, pages 2-3: Brewster, England, Separatists, persecuted, Netherlands, Leiden, banned, children, voted, emigrate, Bradford, Pilgrim, settlers, history, governor, leadership, Bottom of page 3: above, answers will vary, answer will vary

Page 5: 1. unto the Lord; 2. with gladness; 3. with singing; 4. of his pasture; 5. with thanksgiving; 6. with praise; 7. to all generations. Bottom of page: before his; into his; into his

Lesson 2, page 7:

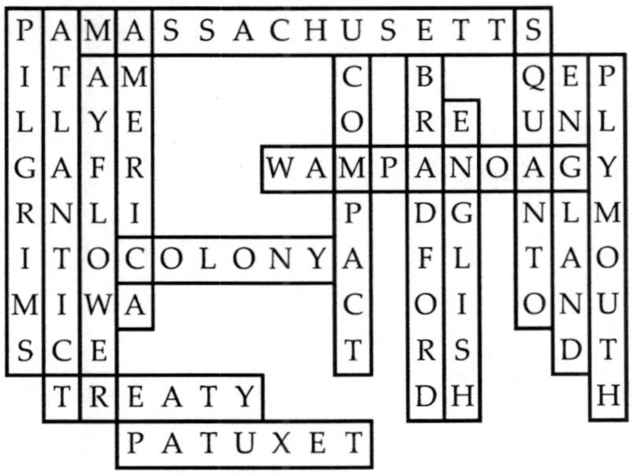

Page 8: rice, wheat, grain, stem, stalk, ear, kernels, cob, food, chips, shells, flakes, meal

Lesson 3, pages 10-11: Plymouth, southern, English, harbor, Pilgrims sailed, Plymouth, historic sailing, sailed, Plymouth, South, Spain, Plymouth, Sir, Spain, Spanish, ships, Spanish, set sail, Plymouth, Spanish, planes, Plymouth, Invasion, sailed, sailed, important, Plymouth, Passenger, Plymouth, fishing port, Plymouth, Plymouth, population

Page 13:

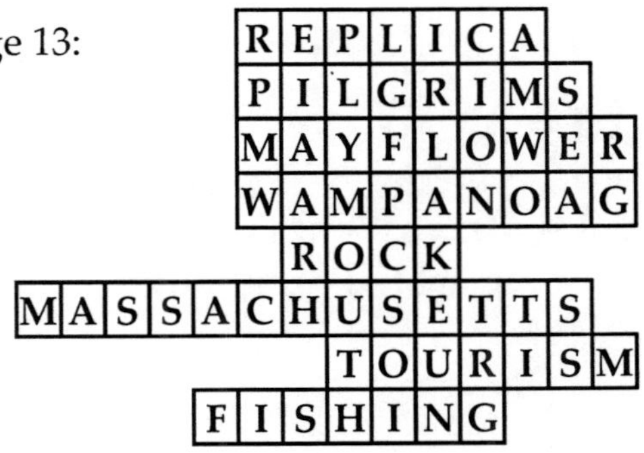

Lesson 4, page 14: autumn, Pilgrims, Plymouth, harvest, Governor, hunting, fowl, feasting, recreation, tribe, Chief, celebration, deer, gifts

Page 17:

Lesson 5, page 19: gather, chastens, hastens, cease, sing, winning, wast, extol, pray, praised; Chasten - to correct, to discipline; Extol - to praise highly

Page 20: A. Forever, B. In a fish, C. Anna, D. Toward heaven, E. A Samaritan, F. Cup, G. Thanksgiving, H. They recognized Jesus.

Page 21: Luke 17:11-19; Luke 2:36-38; Matthew 26:27; Jonah 2:9-10; Luke 24:28-31

Lesson 6, pages 22-23: 1. meeting, 2. turns, 3. food, 4. servants, 5. family, 6. beef, army, 7. venison, pigeon pasties, pork, turkey, goose, 8. pumpkin, tarts, Indian pudding, 9. ballads, 10. hymn, prayer, 11. stories

Page 25: 1. pulp, 2. flowers, 3. seeds, 4. leaves, 5. tendrils, 6. shell

Lesson 7, pages 26-27: nouns that refer to God - Being, Author, Lord, Ruler; words with thank as its root word - thanksgiving, thanks; word with bless as its root word - blessing

Page 28:

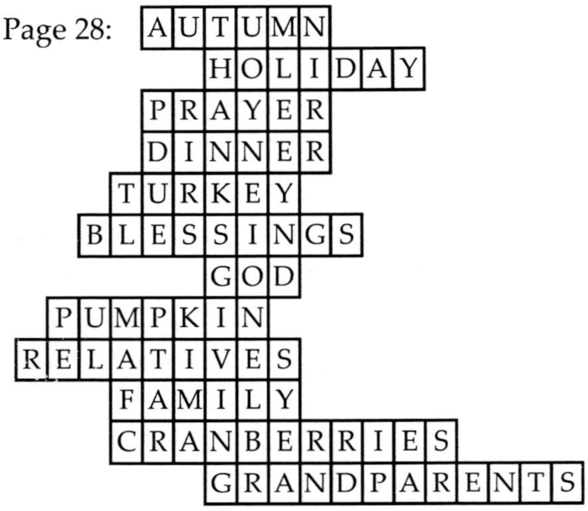

Lesson 8, page 31:

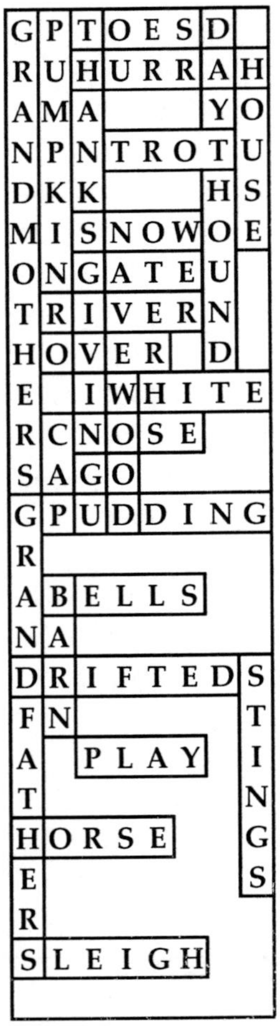

Page 32:

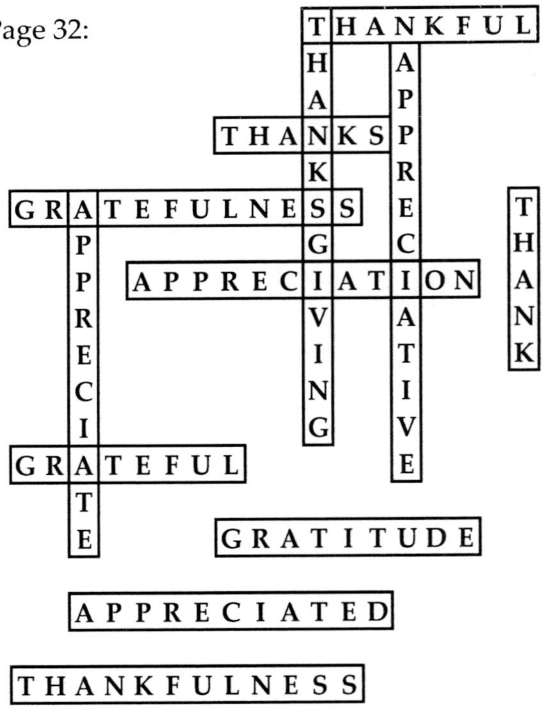

Lesson 9, page 34: New, west, tradition, celebrate, first, Hale, declare, last, each, year

Lesson 10, page 40:

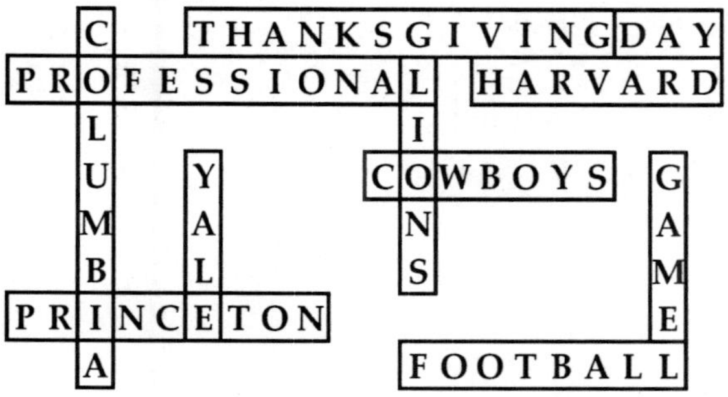

Lesson 11, page 45:

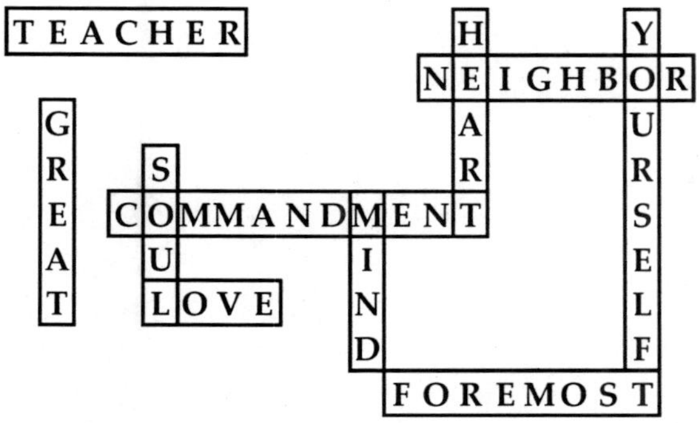

Lesson 14, page 55: Stars and Stripes; Biscuit and Gravy, Marshmallow and Yam; Flyer and Fryer

Lesson 15, page 59:

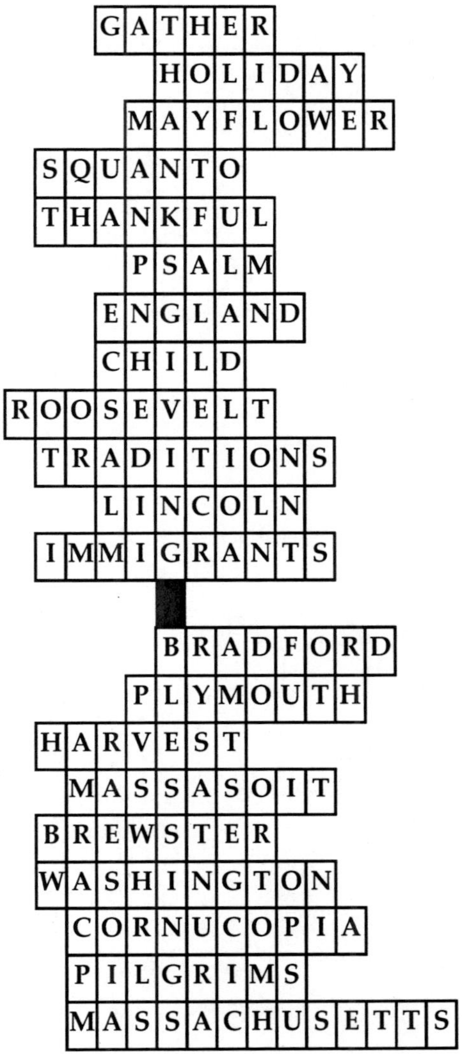

Page 61: Cranbury, Pilgrim, Detroit, fried, car, grown, major, dressing, Capital, hosts

Image Credits

Nova Development Corporation and its licensors — 5, top 6, drawing 8, 16,20, top 23, 29, bottom 30, 32, 48, middle bottom 51, large turkey on page 52, right 57, 65, 71, 82, 83, 90

Library of Congress — photo 27, 36, 38, 40, Harper's magazine cover on page 41, 42, 43, 44, 46, 47, 49, top 51, 53, photos 54, photo 55

Notgrass family photos — introduction photos, back cover, 70

Original drawings by Charlene Notgrass — 65, 72, 73

All other images — JupiterImages.